MW00674458

ANABAP✝IS✝
BEGINNINGS

SWISS & SOUTH GERMAN ANABAPTISTS

LIVING HISTORY THREADS

ANABAPTIST BEGINNINGS: SWISS & SOUTH GERMAN ANABAPTISTS

ISBN 978-0-9816569-6-0

Author: Esther Bean

Photo credits: Bethel College/Mennonite Library and Archives: 33b; Esther Bean: 39b, 41b; Kyle Brubaker: 3, 37; © Herald Press, Scottdale, PA: artwork by Ivan Moon/25, 27, 28, artwork by Oliver Wendell Schenk/10, 12, 13, 22, 24, used by permission; Arlyn Kauffman: 30b, 32, 34a, 36; Marvin Nauman/ FEMA News Photo: 41d; Mennonite Archives of Ontario/Sam Steiner: 41a; nkzs: 7; Emily Turner: 2c, 4c, 24b, 31a, b, 38a, b; Gerald Wagler: 11, 19, 20, 30a; Wikimedia Commons/Creative Commons: Tony Beeman/41c, Dirk Beyer/5b, Andrew Bossi/16-17, Monika Ernst/26b, Roland Fischer/8b, 9, Gadjoboy/40a, b, Gazeta/4a, Thorsten Hartmann/29, Irmgard/4b, it:Utente:TheCadExpert/40d, Hansueli Krapf/4-5, Stefan Kuhn/39c, 42 all, Ad Meskens/39d, Daniel Schwen/6, E. Tinnacher/35, Derek Ramsey/39a; Betty Yoder: 5a, 34b.

Cover design: Kyle Brubaker
Cover picture: *Burning of Maria and Ursula van Beckum, Deventer, 1544* etched by by Jan Luiken

Living History Threads is a history curriculum developed by Faith Builders Resource Group. For more information about Living History Threads, email fbresource@fbep.org or phone 877-222-4769.

Distributed by:
Christian Learning Resource
28500 Guys Mills Road
Guys Mills, PA 16327
www.christianlearning.org
877-222-4769

Copyright © 2010 by Faith Builders Resource Group.

ANABAP†IS†
BEGINNINGS

SWISS & SOUTH GERMAN ANABAPTISTS

Name: _____Ashley_____

School: _____

Grade: ___three___

Everything has a beginning . . .

The day that God
created the world.

The first day of a newly
established country.

The first day of a
school year.

You had a first day too.
When is your birthday?

The group of people known as Anabaptists had a beginning too. This beginning was about five hundred years ago in the country of Switzerland.

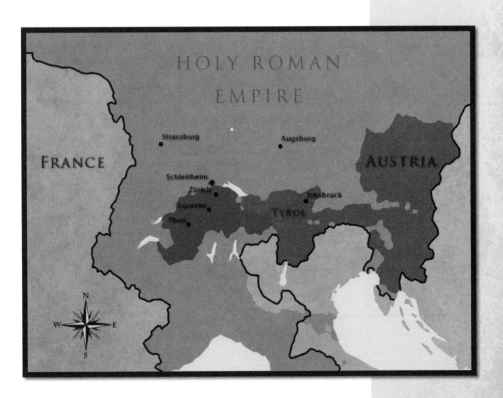

• Alphorn

• Simmental cow

• Chocolate truffles

Switzerland is a dazzlingly beautiful country in Europe known for its mountains, chalets, cowbells, alphorns, and chocolate. It is the country that most of the North American Amish and Mennonites came from a few hundred years ago.

Swiss

landscape

Matterhorn
and Lake
Riffelsee

Swiss chalet

For hundreds of years the state church and the government in Switzerland were joint authorities, working together to control the country. The people were expected to attend the state church's services, agree with its leaders, and fight for its faith. Those who refused were punished.

Village and church of Scuol, Switzerland

Although wealthy people and priests knew how to read, the common people did not. Hardly anyone knew what the Bible actually said. The higher church leaders told the priests what to teach. They did not want people deciding what to believe about ideas such as baptism, war, or communion.

Ulrich Zwingli

Ulrich Zwingli was the priest at the Grossmünster, a church in Zurich, Switzerland. Zwingli saw that changes should be made in the state church. Few priests at this time were able to preach, but Zwingli was a good speaker. Instead of using the church's regular schedule of Sunday readings for his texts, he began to preach straight through the book of Matthew, explaining what he read. This was highly unusual.

Interior of the
Grossmünster

The Grossmünster

Conrad Grebel

Zwingli was not the only one who was reading the Bible and talking about changes. Conrad Grebel, one of Zwingli's students, was also excited about these new ideas.

Conrad Grebel was the son of a wealthy man who served on the city council in Zurich. Grebel had a good education. He had studied in Zurich for six years before attending universities in Switzerland, Austria, and France.

Conrad Grebel lived a wild life as a student. When Grebel's father learned of his disgraceful behavior, he stopped sending him money and told him to come back home.

Conrad Grebel wanted to marry a girl named Barbara. His parents did not approve because she was not from a wealthy, high-class family. When they married anyway, his family was furious.

Grebel began to read the Bible. Soon he knew that he wanted to follow all of God's commands. He became a Christian, and his life changed completely.

Grebel family mansion in Zurich

A number of men, including Grebel, met regularly with Zwingli to read and discuss the Bible. Felix Manz and George Blaurock were also part of this group.

Felix Manz was about twenty-five years old—just like Conrad Grebel. A well-educated man, Manz was a master of Latin, Greek, and Hebrew. His father, a priest, was not married to his mother.

George Blaurock

George Blaurock, a former priest, was an impetuous man with tremendous energy. He was described as tall and powerfully built with fiery eyes, black hair, and a small bald spot. He was called "Blaurock" meaning "blue coat" because he often wore a blue coat.

These men began meeting at night to discuss the Bible. Grebel used the Greek New Testament and Manz used the Hebrew Old Testament to explain what the Bible said. The men saw plainly that the Bible and the teachings of the state church did not agree.

The state church said babies must be baptized. This is called infant baptism. However, the Bible said those who choose to believe and follow Jesus should be baptized. Babies cannot make this choice.

The Bible said people must tell the truth and not swear oaths. The state church asked people to swear oaths to make sure they would tell the truth.

Infant baptism depicted on an altarpiece

The state church forced everyone except the Jews to be part of the church instead of allowing people to choose whether to join the church. Because of this, even ungodly people were church members. The Bible said there should be church discipline. This meant that ungodly people should be warned to change their ways, and that only God-fearing people were to be members of the church.

Fighting against Muslims: Siege of Acre in 1291 (3rd Crusade)

The state church declared war on Muslims (called Turks) and on those who believed differently from the church (heretics). Jesus said that His followers should love their enemies and bless them.

The group with Grebel and Manz decided the state church needed to change. However, Zwingli was not willing to act differently unless the city council agreed. He wanted to wait for changes in the state church until the council was ready.

Disputations were held to try to decide what was right. What did God mean by what He said in the Bible? Zwingli took one side. Grebel, Manz, and a priest named Wilhelm Reublin took the other side.

Zwingli and the council said they must decide what should be believed and preached. The other men said

the Bible had already decided what was right. They also said, "We should obey God rather than men."

At the end of the disputations, the council announced a decision. All babies must be baptized within eight days of their birth, or the family would be banished from the canton. The Bible classes must end, and the men must stop disputing. Four men were banished from Zurich.

Courthouse (far left) and Grossmünster (two towers) by Limmat River in Zurich

On January 21, 1525, a group of fifteen men met at the home of Felix Manz's mother. It was an illegal meeting, but they wanted to pray together and discuss how to deal with the council's law requiring infant baptism.

As they prayed, the men felt that God was moving in their hearts. They asked God to help them do His will.

Following the prayer, George Blaurock stood up and asked Conrad Grebel to baptize him with a true Christian baptism as a believer. Blaurock knelt, and Grebel baptized him. Then the others asked Blaurock to baptize them, which he did. This was the beginning of the Anabaptist church.

The group started small, but the results were felt all over Switzerland. The men began preaching and teaching in Zurich and other towns nearby. They held services in homes, in fields, and in the woods. Blaurock even marched into two churches and announced that he was sent by God to preach instead of the regular priest.

These Anabaptist leaders were educated and could write well. They explained their beliefs and tried to persuade others about the truth.

Street of the house in which the first Anabaptists were rebaptized

These beliefs became very popular; many were drawn to this new church. Those who wished to join asked for baptism. Sometimes three hundred people were baptized in one place!

People who were loyal to the state church began to call this new group "Anabaptists," meaning "rebaptizers." It was a nasty name, and the new group did not like it, but the name stuck.

The state church saw Anabaptists as rebellious people who were stealing their church members. They arrested many Anabaptists, threw them into prison, and tried to persuade them to give up their faith.

Courthouse
on the
Limmat River

Some people did recant. They said they would listen to Zwingli and the council.

The council tried to arrest the leaders and force the Anabaptist movement to stop. Grebel, Manz, and Blaurock were captured and sentenced to prison on a diet of gruel, bread, and water. No visitors were allowed.

In spite of this treatment, the men refused to change their beliefs unless they would be shown in the Bible that they were wrong. They managed to escape and kept right on preaching. Some of the leaders were arrested several times.

In 1526 the first leader of the Anabaptists died. A terrible disease called the plague was killing people at that time. Conrad Grebel was not in good health, due to his former wild lifestyle.

Grebel was less than thirty years old when he died, but because of his leadership, he became known as the Father of Anabaptists.

Felix Manz was the first Anabaptist of the original group to be martyred. The state church was frustrated with the Anabaptists' refusal to obey. They hoped that if one was killed, the rest would become scared and recant. Two days before Manz was killed, Zwingli wrote in a letter, "The Anabaptist, who should already have been sent to the devil, disturbs the peace of the pious people. But I believe the ax will settle it."

On January 5, 1527, Felix Manz was taken out of prison and led to the fish market, where his death sentence was read. "Manz shall be delivered to the executioner, who shall tie his hands, put him into a boat, take him to the lower hut,

Drowning of
Felix Manz

there strip his bound hands down over his knees, place a stick between his knees and arms, and thus push him into the water, and let him perish."

He was taken to the Limmat River and placed in a boat with the executioner and a priest. Many people lined the river to see the drowning. Felix Manz's mother and brother shouted encouragement to him.

He was rowed to a small fishing hut in the middle of the river. As Manz was being bound, he sang, "Lord, into Your hands I commend my spirit."

Then Felix Manz was pushed into the cold waters of the Limmat River and died as an Anabaptist martyr.

On the same day, George Blaurock was taken out of prison and punished. He was stripped to the waist and beaten with rods as he was expelled from the city.

This treatment did not dampen Blaurock's passion. He continued preaching, especially in the Tyrol area of Austria. It is estimated that he won a thousand converts in the short time before he was arrested again. In September of 1529, George Blaurock was burned at the stake near Innsbruck, Austria.

River Inn,
Innsbruck,
Austria

Michael Sattler lived in southern Germany and held a high position in a monastery. He was appalled at the sinful behavior of monks, so he left the monastery and married a woman named Margaretha.

Sattler traveled to Zurich, joined the Anabaptists in 1525, and was banished from Zurich. Soon after Felix Manz's death, he was in charge at a meeting near Schleitheim, on the border between Switzerland and Germany.

Title page of
Schleitheim
Confession

Schleitheim,
Switzerland

The Anabaptists wanted to have a written copy of their beliefs—a confession of faith. Michael Sattler compiled ideas and wrote the Schleitheim Confession. It listed the most important aspects of what the Anabaptists believed, such as baptism, communion, separation from the world, and nonresistance. It gave instructions for how new leaders should be chosen if pastors were imprisoned or killed.

The state church was determined to kill this Anabaptist leader too. They arrested Michael Sattler, his wife, and several others. They were held in prison until their court trial.

At the trial, Sattler spoke of his beliefs. Some men at the trial became so angry that they volunteered to kill Sattler by themselves. Finally the verdict was read. The executioner was to cut out Michael Sattler's tongue. Then he was to hurt Sattler's body terribly seven times before burning him to death as a heretic.

These tortures were unspeakably horrible, but Sattler remained true to his faith. He even prayed for his persecutors and praised God as he died.

Pilgram Marpeck

Pilgram Marpeck was one of the most unusual of the early Anabaptist leaders. He was not a priest, but was well trained as a mining engineer. He was elected to the city council and was a mine magistrate.

He felt that the Anabaptists were true to the Scriptures. When he joined them in 1528, he was expelled from his position and his property was confiscated.

He found safety in Strassburg, Germany (now France), where he served for several years as a civil engineer. He baptized people and formed a church. When he was banished from Strassburg, he moved to Augsburg.

From 1544 to 1556, he worked as an engineer for the city of Augsburg. Pilgram Marpeck was a good leader and writer. Some of his writings may be read today. They help us to know what Anabaptists believed.

The city officials did not like Marpeck's Anabaptist activities. However, they felt he was too valuable to the city to kill, so they let him continue until he died a natural death.

Stream near
Augsburg,
Germany

The state church and the government of Switzerland used many methods to try to force people to recant. They threw them into prisons where the conditions were terrible. Swiss Anabaptists were kept in the castle in Thun and in the dungeons in Lucerne.

Tower with dungeons in Lucerne

Castle in Thun

Many prisoners were held in Trachselwald
Castle in Switzerland.

Barred window in
Trachselwald Castle

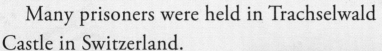

Stocks and chains in
Trachselwald Castle

Torture
rack

Anabaptists were tortured horribly to get them to recant or to give information about other Anabaptists. A common torture instrument was the rack, where people would be slowly stretched, causing severe pain. Another method was to tighten screws on thumbs, fingers, or knees. God was with the believers in these terrible experiences and gave them strength and courage.

If tortures did not work, the Anabaptists were sentenced to death. Altogether in Switzerland, Germany, and Holland, between four and five thousand Anabaptists were killed in about one hundred years.

Burning at the stake in Amsterdam

Drowning of Maria van Monjou

Certainly the Anabaptists were in great danger. They were bold and courageous, but facing torture and death was frightening.

Tauferhohle
(Anabaptist Cave)

Some leaders were continually on the run. They held church services wherever they could— in a barn, in the woods, on a boat, in a cave. These pictures show a cave in Switzerland where Anabaptists hid and held services.

An Early Church leader, Tertullian, had said, "The blood of the martyrs is the seed of the church."

About 350 Anabaptists were killed in Alzey in 1529. The Count of Alzey said something similar to Tertullian's words. He exclaimed, "What shall I do? The more I kill, the greater becomes their number!"

Castle in Alzey

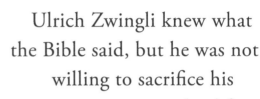

Ulrich Zwingli knew what the Bible said, but he was not willing to sacrifice his reputation or his life to stand up for what was right. He died fighting in a battle near Zurich.

Outside the Wasserkirche in Zurich, there is a statue of Ulrich Zwingli. Look closely at the picture. Do you see him holding a sword and a Bible? How does that seem to fit his life?

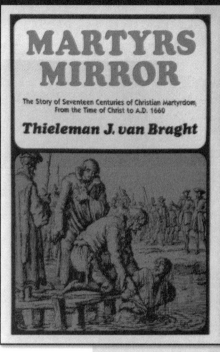

MARTYRS MIRROR

The Story of Seventeen Centuries of Christian Martyrdom, From the Time of Christ to A.D. 1660

Thieleman J. van Braght

The *Martyrs Mirror* is a large book containing many stories of Christians who have died for their faith. In this book you can read of martyrs in the Early Church. You can also find stories of Swiss and German Anabaptists, such as Leonard Keyser, whose body, and the flower he was holding, did not burn. There is a fascinating poem about Hans Haslibacher's three unusual signs that he was innocent. A large section of the book is about Dutch Anabaptists such as Dirk Willems and Elizabeth Dirks. Maybe your parents or grandparents have a copy of *Martyrs Mirror*.

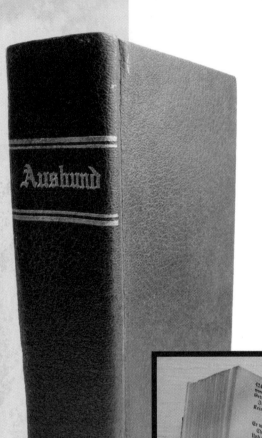

If you know German, you can read poems in the *Ausbund*. The *Ausbund* is a collection of songs written by martyrs.

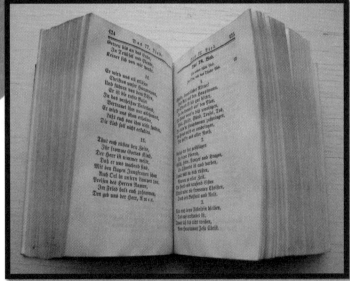

• Amish buggy

• Mennonite girl

• Hutterite children

Anabaptists continue to this day. Maybe your family is part of an Anabaptist church. Often Anabaptists are known by other names, such as Amish, Mennonite, or Hutterite.

Dairy farm
owned by Amish

Amish

- Amish farmer

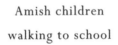

Amish children
walking to school

- Horse and buggy

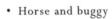

Mennonites

• Old Order Mennonite church

Mennonites helping
clean up after a
disaster in Louisiana

• Mennonites on the New River, Belize

Hutterites

• Sign for Hutterite colony

• Youth singing

HUTTERIAN BRETHREN
OAK BLUFF COLONY
MORRIS, MAN.

• Husking corn

• Girls washing dishes

New buildings for
a Hutterite colony